Overcomer

by the blood of the lamb and the word of my testimony

Overcomer

by the blood of the lamb and the word of my testimony

Joyce A. Hawkins

WESTBOW
PRESS
A DIVISION OF THOMAS NELSON

WestBow Press books may be ordered through booksellers or by contacting:
WestBow Press
A Division of Thomas Nelson
1663 Liberty Drive
Bloomington, IN 47403
www.westbowpress.com
1-(866) 928-1240

ISBN: 978-1-4497-0867-2 (sc)
ISBN: 978-1-4497-0866-5 (e)

Library of Congress Control Number: 2001012345

Printed in the United States of America

WestBow Press rev. date: 12/15/2010

Dedicated To

My daughters, Judy and Jackie

Acknowledgments

Bishop Bergeta G. Allen who was strong enough
to "stir the nest" and make me fly

Rev. Phyllis Anderson who saw my pain and encouraged me by
giving me hugs and holding my hand as I regained stability

Dr. Spencer Johnson, sent by God to walk
with me through the dark hours

Introduction

My journey to becoming an overcomer had to be made on a road that was strewn with tests and trials. I thank God for every minute of it. Without opposition, I would not have developed any warring tools to confront the obstacles in my path, and I would not have this testimony.

Everything I have gone through to experience this book was well worth the struggle. The first time I read Romans 8:18, I did not understand what the scripture was saying—but now I am telling the world, whatever trials I faced were necessary. No hurt, disappointment, sickness, or sorrow will ever be visible through the light of God's Glory, which shines through me.

I found in order to triumph over everyday trials and tribulations, I had to believe everything would be okay. However, my faith was lying dormant; I had almost no trust in God. To build a relationship with God, I first had to understand that without faith, I would never be able to please Him. Then I wondered how could I depend on God, when I know I am not pleasing Him? The guilt of my shortcoming would not allow me to trust Him fully.

As I built more and more trust, I began to develop patience as I learned to wait for God's timing. Along with building trust and developing patience, I needed to learn (and I am still learning) to hear God.

If you find yourself close to the state I was in, you will find something in this book that will help you deal with your situation; something to encourage your understanding of what it means to fight and war in the spirit to overcome the adversary; something to help you be at peace with God and yourself.

As you read of my trials and ultimate victory, my prayer for you is that you understand that although trials are uncomfortable as they are experienced, they are good for building muscle in the spirit. God bless you as you read on—

Just to be sure we are all on the same page concerning things that please God, I decided to share Chapter 11 of Hebrews from the Living Bible Translation with you. The examples mentioned here are the standards I used to measure faith throughout this book.

Hebrews 11

What is faith? It is the confident assurance that something we want is going to happen. It is the certainty that what we hope for is waiting for us, even though we cannot see it up ahead. Men of God in days of old were famous for their faith.

By faith—by believing God—we know that the world and the stars— in fact, all things—were made at God's command; and that they were all made from things that cannot be seen.

*It was by faith that **Abel** obeyed God and brought an offering that pleased God more than Cain's offering did. God accepted Abel and proved it by accepting his gift; and though Abel is long dead, we can still learn lessons from him about trusting God.*

***Enoch** trusted God too, and that is why God took him away to heaven without dying; suddenly he was gone because God took Him. Before this happened God had said how pleased he was with Enoch. You can never please God without faith, without depending on him. Anyone who wants to come to God must believe that there is a God and that he rewards those who sincerely look for him.*

***Noah** was another who trusted God. When he heard God's warning about the future, Noah believed him even though there was then no sign of a flood, and wasting no time, he built the ark and saved his family. Noah's belief in God was in direct contrast to the sin and disbelief of the rest of the world—which refused to obey— and because of his faith he became one of those who God has accepted.*

Abraham trusted God, and when God told him to leave home and go far away to another land which he promised to give him, Abraham obeyed. Away he went, not even knowing where he was going. And even when he reached God's promised land, he lived in tents like a mere visitor, as did Isaac and Jacob, to whom God gave the same promise. Abraham did this because he was confidently waiting for God to bring him to that strong heavenly city whose designer and builder is God.

Sarah, too, had faith, and because of this she was able to become a mother in spite of her old age, for she realized that God who gave her his promise, would certainly do what he said. And so a whole nation came from Abraham, who was too old to have even one child—a nation with so many millions of people that, like the stars of the sky and the sand on the ocean shores, that there is no way to count them.

These men of faith I have mentioned died without ever receiving all that god had promised them; but they saw it all awaiting them on ahead and were glad, for they agreed that this earth was not their real home but that they were just strangers visiting down here. And quite obviously when they talked like that, they were looking forward to their real home in heaven. If they had wanted to, they could have gone back to the good things of this world. But they did not want to. They were living for heaven. And now God is not ashamed to be called their God, for he has made a heavenly city for them.

While God was testing him, Abraham still trusted in God and his promises, and so he offered up his son Isaac, and was ready to slay him on the alter of sacrifice; yes, to slay even Isaac, through whom God had promised to give Abraham a whole nation of descendants!

He believed that if Isaac died God would bring him back to life again; and that is just about what happened, for as far as Abraham was concerned, Isaac was doomed to death, but he came back again alive! It was by faith that *Isaac* knew God would give future blessings to his two sons, Jacob and Esau.

By faith *Jacob*, when he was old and dying, blessed each of Joseph's two sons as he stood and prayed, leaning on the top of his cane. And it was by faith that *Joseph*, as he neared the end of his life, confidently spoke of God bringing the people of Israel out of Egypt; and he was so sure of it that he made them promise to carry his bones with them when they left!

Moses' parents had faith too. When they say that God had given them an unusual child, they trusted that God would save him from the death the king commanded, and they hid him for three months, and were not afraid.

It was by faith that **Moses**, when he grew up, refused to be treated as the grandson of the king, but chose to share ill-treatment with God's people instead of enjoying the fleeting pleasures of sin. He thought that was better to suffer for the promised Christ than to own all the treasures of Egypt, for he was looking forward to the great reward that God would give him. And it was because he trusted God that he left the land of Egypt and wasn't afraid of the king's anger. Moses kept right on going; it seemed as though he could see God right there with him. And it was because he believed God would save his people that he commanded them to kill a lamb as God had told them to and sprinkle the blood on the doorposts of their homes, so that God's terrible Angel of Death could not touch the oldest child in those homes, as he did among the Egyptians.

The **people of Israel** trusted God and went right through the Red Sea as though they were on dry ground. But when the Egyptians chasing them tried it, they all were drowned. It was faith that brought the walls of Jericho tumbling down after the people of Israel had walked around them seven days, as God had commanded them.

By faith—because she believed in God and his power—**Rahab** the harlot did not die with all the others in her city when they refused to obey God, for she gave a friendly welcome to the spies.

Well, how much more do I need to say? It would take too long to recount the stores of the faith of **Gideon** and **Barak** and **Samson** and **Jephthah** and **David** and **Samuel** and all the other prophets. These people all trusted God and as a result won battles, overthrew kingdoms, ruled their people well, and received what God had promised them; they were kept from harm in a den of lions, and in a fiery furnace. Some, through their faith, escaped death by the sword. Some were made strong again after they had been weak or sick. Others were given great power in battle; they made whole armies turn and run away.

And some women, through faith, received their loved ones back again from death. But others trusted God and were beaten to death, preferring to die rather than turn from God and be free—trusting that they would rise to a better life afterwards.

Some were laughed at and their backs cut open with whips, and others were chained in dungeons. Some died by stoning and some by being sawed in two; others were promised freedom if they would renounce their faith, then were killed with the sword.

Some went about in skins of sheep and goats, wandering over deserts and mountains, hiding in dens and caves. They were hungry and sick and ill-treated—too good for this world.

And these men of faith, though they trusted God and won his approval, none of them received all that God had promised them; for God wanted them to wait and share the even better rewards that were prepared for us.

– Hebrews 11:1-40 TLB

Part 1

Life's tests always turn
into Testimonies so...

My brethren, count it all joy when ye fall into divers temptations;

Knowing this, that the trying of your faith worketh patience.

But let patience have her perfect work, that ye may be perfect and entire, wanting nothing.

– James 1:2-4 (KJV)

Keep the Faith

As Christians, we must have confident assurance that God is going to come through for us; we must have faith that God will do what He has promised us as heirs of Abraham. When times get hard and we realize we cannot handle a situation, whatever it is, we must trust God for the solution. All too often, we forget we have access to the ultimate source, and we fret over situations—sometimes for extended periods. We suffer agony and irritation unnecessarily, because our faith muscle is weak: weak faith indicates a lack of trust in God. It is at this point of our need that our faith should be strong. It should be so deeply embedded in us that no matter what challenge we face, we remember God is ready, willing, and able. We must realize that we determine how far we will allow God to go for us.

God is limitless. We put Him in a box, thereby limiting His creativity in our lives. Does He not say in His word that without the Holy Spirit, our little minds are not capable of conceiving the magnitude of His plan for our lives? When we love the Lord and invite the Holy Spirit to be an active part of our lives, our minds expand, and we can get a glimpse of His plan for us. That is how we take the limits off God.

Faith examined

Life without faith in God trusts something that is not reliable. Think about it. Without faith in God you could fall into trusting in fate, destiny, even self-reliance. For example, faith in destiny may not allow you to believe you could go to your mailbox without something horrible happening. You might not be able to leave your house because of fear. You know that is not of God because the scripture tells us so.

"For God has not given us a spirit of fear but of power and of love and of a sound mind."

– 2 Timothy 1:7 NKJV

Faith is needed on many levels for everyday living. Let's look at crossing the street. You have, without thinking about it, confident assurance you will be able to cross a busy street without being hurt. However, you can only hope you will be okay. It is impossible to know with 100 percent certainty whether the approaching car or truck will actually stop at the traffic light and allow you to cross the street safely. Faith says, God in His infinite goodness enabled the vehicle to operate properly and allow you to cross safely. That example is a simple demonstration of faith. It is exactly that kind of faith though—faith without reservation—that we need in larger, more complex situations. Acknowledging that it is God, who controls everything, makes it easier to see what faith in God can do.

Faith is also like pouring water on a dry sponge. Try it. You will see how the sponge expands to a far greater size than it appeared when dry. Notice the expansion is directly related to how much water is poured on the sponge. Just as the sponge expands according to the amount of water added, your faith will expand, according to how much you believe God controls. Just as the water on the sponge begins to expand the sponge, the level of your belief that God controls everything starts that mustard seed-sized faith to increase.

I have no formula for building your faith muscle. The more you believe God is able, that He wants to be there for you, and that He is only waiting for you to believe, the more confident you will become. I can only offer my personal experiences to try to help you see how my faith in God has made my life so much more bearable. In difficult times, when I call on God, my circumstance may not change. On the other hand, my *outlook* is always changed when I remember God controls vast amounts of resources.

My journey

My husband Jim, and I had always gone to church, paid our tithes, participated in praise and worship, and acted and looked like a fine Christian family. Each of us had influence over many people with whom we came in contact daily. These people watched our every move and were impressed by what the natural eye could see. When others would cry and plead with God to help them by approving mortgage loans, car loans, and other such material gain, I never did. My stand was always that Jim and I want that, please God, give it to us. I would leave it there, and He never failed me. There did not seem to be anything we wanted that God did not permit us to have. I did not realize at the time, but our faith muscles were about to be exercised.

One night at a church service, I bumped into a prophet of God. His anointing pushed me to the floor, and life, literally, has not been the same since. The prophet's word from God for me was:

- Everyone bearing my name would be saved.
- As of midnight, I would receive a complete transfusion.

I stayed up until midnight waiting for a sign of transformation. No visible change occurred. The next morning, I was quite disappointed. I could not see a difference, and I did not feel any different. I did not know what I was expecting; a blood transfusion would not be evident to the naked eye!

About a year later, Jim and I were in a service at our church; the sermon topic was "Launch out into the deep. " It was as if we both got the message at the same time. The preacher said we should take a leap forward and repeat, "Launch out into the deep". Jim grabbed my hand and said, "Let's launch out". Ordinarily he was not one to follow preachers when they ask the congregation to "Turn to your neighbor and say . . . ". I joined him gladly as we took a leap forward. With that step, we began a search for a more acceptable life in Christ.

Game Changers

Jim developed an ulcer on one of his toes. Being a type two diabetic made this a serious situation. I initially thought amputation was inevitable. You may rest assured we acknowledged God as Jehovah Rapha and partitioned His healing power. However, before we had time to beg God for healing, Jim had been hospitalized and surgery performed. As it turned out, our podiatrist was able to scrape the bone and save his toe. When the toe was healed, there wasn't even a scar. Thank God, amputation was not necessary. For Jim, that would have been difficult because he was a hair stylist-he routinely stood more than eight hours, five days a week. After the surgery, his doctor insisted he stay off the foot for six weeks. Oh, my God, six weeks, no income for six weeks!

That break in Jim's income was the first assault on our finances. Not being better prepared, financially, for a time when Jim would not be working was a prime example of our NOT looking to God for instructions.

I let a bothersome manager rush me into retirement. If I had asked God for His direction, He would have ordered my steps, and I probably would not have retired when I did. From a physical standpoint, I could have worked another ten to fifteen years. From a mental standpoint, another ten days would have been extremely hard.

A month after retiring, before I had recuperated from the pressures of the old job, from out of nowhere, one of our creditors decided we were not paying our bills in a timely enough fashion. The creditor canceled our membership and demanded payment in full on all our accounts. We had several lines of credit with the company and had been members with the same payment record for more than twenty years.

Then, in less than six months after retiring, the roof on our home had to be replaced. Jim's earnings plus my retirement annuity (and no credit cards) was not sufficient to allow us to continue the high standard of living as before. I took a job at a TV station in its Information Technology (IT) department. The pay was good enough to get credit to have the roof replaced. Jim's illness was taking its toll on him and he could not work long hours as he had in the past. Nevertheless, we were doing OK, but still not looking to God for advice on anything.

Looking back, I still do not understand how both Jim and I missed the scripture that admonishes us to acknowledge God in all our ways and promises if we do, He will direct our paths. We only acknowledged Him after we failed.

Calm before the storm

> *"So, if you think you are standing firm, be careful that you don't fall! No temptation has seized you except what is common to man. And God is faithful; he will not let you be tempted beyond what you can bear. But when you are tempted, he will also provide a way out so that you can stand up under it."*
>
> *– 1 Corinthians 10:12-13 NIV*

Life was stressful. Jim and I needed a vacation. Jim's illnesses and tender feet were slowing him down and I was just plain tired. Jim's Cousin Mildred and her husband, John, were planning a trip to Bermuda with his Kiwanis Club. Because it was with his club, he could assure us it was not too late to arrange for us to come along. Looking back, that trip was the honeymoon Jim and I opted not to take at the beginning of our life together. It was peaceful, restorative, and relaxing.

Jim did not normally wear a tie to work but he loved getting dressed. Dressing for dinner each night was right up his alley, he loved it. Just that simple little thing took his mind off his illness and did wonders for his spirit. The Bible says laughter is good medicine and that trip made me a believer. John, Mildred, Jim and I spent hours sitting and reflecting on times past with such joy. We laughed often, remembering how carefree and uncomplicated life was years ago.

One week after the Bermuda cruise, Jim fell and broke his hip. The outlook for recovery was good, but we expected him to be out of work for at least two months. He needed hip replacement surgery. There was no delay in healing because of diabetes. However, because of diabetes, ulcers began to form on the heels of his feet.

Rough seas ahead! While Jim was still recuperating, the entire IT department at the TV station where I worked was outsourced. I was given three weeks notice and a very small severance. I decided not to look for another job but to stay home with Jim instead. In reality, the timing was perfect. I did not know it then, but Jim was going to need me at home.

While I was still wandering through the rose garden, Jim had gotten it, he knew what he had to do and he did it. He worked on getting closer to God, though I remained clueless. He had taken the leap.

Let's see now, debts were mounting; there was not enough income; we had very little money in reserve; Jim was becoming more and more ill and looking less and less like he would ever be able to work again.

The faith that seemed to work for me on automatic began to diminish. Talk about a weak faith muscle! Not only was it weak, I had no idea how to strengthen it. I had no idea what horrible shape I was in. Could anyone else on this planet be as insensitive to the Holy Spirit as I? Still not seeing; still not hearing; still not talking to God with any consistency!

My allegiance to God was limited to Sunday morning service—two hours weekly. I was not even a midweek Bible study regular. I did nothing to serve anyone. I was giving my tithes and offerings. That was one of the few things I was doing that was pleasing to God.

When I was a child, I remember hearing people at church say, "God has a way that is mighty sweet"—it sounded silly to me then but now I understand. Sometimes God places us in situations that leave us no choice but to seek Him and that is "mighty sweet" of Him.

As I worried and fretted, I began to realize, God is my source and I need to trust Him completely. I had to face the problems head-on, knowing God is in control. There was nothing I could do except talk to Him about everything; tell Him about my fears concerning my husband, my home and my stability. I had to hold His hand.

By holding God's hand, relying on Him for everything, I was acknowledging His control and my mustard seed-sized faith expanded with each trial. As spiritually slow as I was, I knew the danger in letting go. I began to develop a real confident assurance that God was going to take care of everything we were facing—debts, illness and my serious lack of spiritual direction. The path on which I had been placed was far too difficult to travel without God, I had no desire to turn around, and I would not backup!

Part 2

When hard times seem to
want to knock you down...

And let us not lose heart and grow weary and faint in acting nobly and doing right, for in due time and at the appointed season we shall reap, if we do not loosen and relax our courage and faint

— Galatians 6:9 AMP

Don't backup

Peter walked on water until he realized what he was doing, and then he began to sink. Jesus was there and offered His hand. In that instant, Peter was rescued. Peter knew if he could reach the Masters hand, he would not sink further. Peter did not wonder if God was willing, or if Jesus would come to his aid, he believed safety was in his reach—in Jesus' hand.

The same is true of the Woman with the issue of blood—she knew Jesus could heal her and she did not wonder if He would. The woman knew if she could get to Jesus, even touch his robe, she would be healed. And she was, not in the next hour, day, or week, but instantly as she crawled through the crowd, on the ground, and touched the hem of His robe.

If Peter or the woman had backed away from their belief in Jesus and his healing power, Peter could have drowned and the woman could have continued to be an outcast for the rest of her life. Thank You Jesus, they did not backup!

Although Jim and I never talked about our doubts, we had the same fears and concerns. *Would* God restore the circulation in his feet and legs? *Was God willing* to do it, I knew He could, but *would* He? How long would it take? Did Jim need to *believe*, along with me, that he was already healed? Yes, he did indeed have to believe he was healed by the stripes to Jesus' body. God would have restored the circulation to Jim's feet the instant he accepted the healing. Accepting and believing was not something I could do for him.

The key to obtaining confident assurance of things hoped for but not seen, is to understand that God does not consider anything about our past or our imperfection. When we ask for deliverance or healing from

God, we seldom really believe it will happen because deep within, we know how unworthy we are. We know what we did last night. We know why we feel so stressed. We know it would serve us right to remain in the state we are in—we worked hard for it and we deserve it!

Thank you Jesus! God does not think like that. There are no extenuating circumstances that would not allow our healing or deliverance. God is not interested in making us pay for the wrong we have done. Oh, we will pay, but our paying is not His focus. He will not punish us with infirmities and illnesses because of wrong decisions or even willful disobedience. When we ask, He will forgive all our sins.

Certainly, Jim and I had cause for pause in asking God for help after we ignored Him so thoroughly in the past. This self-condemnation could have prevented us from the deliverance we finally received. Thank you Jesus, we learned that God does not condemn those of us who are in Christ Jesus. Romans 8 tells us this.

Like many people, we just assumed going to church and doing busy work was all we needed to do. Not so, God requires a consistent lifestyle that represents Him. Isaiah 57 is clear about the benefits of works when one has worshiped idols and ignored God:

> *"Whom have you so dreaded and feared*
> *that you have been false to me,*
> *and have neither remembered me*
> *nor pondered this in your hearts?*
> *Is it not because I have long been silent*
> *that you do not fear me?*
>
> *I will expose your righteousness and your works,*
> *and they will not benefit you.*
>
> *When you cry out for help,*
> *let your collection of idols save you!*
> *The wind will carry all of them off,*
> *a mere breath will blow them away.*
> *But the man who makes me his refuge*
> *will inherit the land*
> *and possess my holy mountain."*
>
> *– Isaiah 57:11-13 NIV*

The decision to do it God's way, through a consistent lifestyle is what carried us. Consistency is what allowed us to keep moving forward and not backing up when doctors insisted on amputation of his right foot. Naturally, we were devastated but I was still looking to God for a miracle. We waited on Him and Jim possessed His holy mountain.

Jim's right leg healed quickly. However, the other foot was not doing well, and the diabetes was wreaking havoc on his kidneys. Periodically, trying to save the left foot, doctors would scrape the wound to rid it of infected tissue. With each scraping, the wound grew larger and larger. The last time they treated the wound; they took him to surgery and removed all of the fleshy tissue that remained on his heel. When they finished, bone was exposed. I suppose this was their way of telling us:

"you will agree to amputate this foot now!"

Deliverance

Somewhere in the back of my mind, I always knew God was controlling everything. He definitely orchestrated my job at the TV station. I asked Him for that job because I liked the idea of working for a Black owned company with young African-American professionals. He had other ideas. The experience was wonderful though. My association with my manager led to an important deliverance for me.

For my entire life, I suffered from what I will call a weak stomach. I could not even bear to see mutilated carcasses (road kill) on the street. I attributed this condition to watching my brother smash a turtle with a big rock. I can still see its blood and entrails. Whether killing the turtle was a boy thing or if it was done for shock value, I do not know.

For several months after, I could not eat tomato soup, a staple in my sensitive stomach diet as a child. I should have known better than to play with him because he never wanted me around. I guess a nine-year-old boy and a five-year-old girl do not make the best playmates—but he was my big brother and I felt privileged he wanted to spend time with me.

One day as my manager and I were having lunch at a Chinese restaurant, the subject of mice came up. You see, my manager was looking for new living quarters and the most recent house she visited had been vacant for a while. She found evidence of mice! I told her about my aversion to mice and how I could not eat for days after seeing a mouse or sensing their presence. Even talking about them was upsetting to me.

Well, wouldn't you know, her conversation immediately turned to mice. She even said she saw one go behind the booth across from us. You know it; I could not finish lunch and could not eat dinner either.

God did it again! I was so accustomed to the weak stomach syndrome it did not occur to me to pray for healing or deliverance. I am not sure I even considered the condition demonically influenced. But, Hallelujah! Glory to God! Thank You, Jesus! I was completely delivered the next morning. As I showered, I could feel the oppression washing down the drain. I felt a lightness I had never felt. I thought I would float right out of the shower. I experienced a freedom in my head I will never be able to describe.

My manager and I lunched together daily so when it was time for lunch, I suggested we go to the restaurant where we had lunch the day before. As we ordered our food, I told her of the new freedom and lightness I was feeling. She did not appreciate my deliverance nearly as much as I did. I may be exaggerating, but I do not think she could eat her lunch! Her mission had been accomplished. For one reason or another, we never had lunch together after that.

That was my first experience as an overcomer by the blood of the Lamb and the word of my testimony. By His blood, I was healed and delivered. When I told my manager of my healing, that was my testimony. I needed that healing for work yet to be done.

The first time I changed the bandage and saw his foot, my sight dimmed and I almost fainted. I could not have managed to work with Jim's wounds, changing bloody bandages, cleaning wounds with fatty tissue exposed, and rewrapping them if I had not been delivered from my weak stomach several months before. God is good! He has always provided for me before I even knew what I was going to need.

Our podiatrist is a friend of the family and lives just a few doors up the street from us. I called her and asked her to come by to see Jim's foot. I wanted her opinion about him going to Switzerland. I had already warned her about the wound so as she unwrapped his foot, she held her breath to keep from gasping but there was nothing she could do about the tears that fell. It was good Jim could not see his wound or us.

Some dreams do come true

Jim was invited to sing at the Chéserex Jazz Festival in Montreux, Switzerland. In less than two months, a dream he had pursued for some time, could come true. Now that it was in his reach, it seemed as though he would miss the opportunity. He became depressed and gave up on the trip. He suggested the girls go without him. He always referred to our daughters, Judy, Jackie and our goddaughter, Cynthia as "the girls". They sang backup with him many years. They could have gone without him. Their harmony is beautifully blended, and they sing with an anointing that demands attention. Europeans love Gospel singing as an art form so they appreciate beautiful voices and style, qualities the girls have.

Time for the trip was drawing near; Jim was in the hospital when the tickets and itinerary arrived. We thought the tickets would boost his spirit. As we talked about the trip at the hospital, we tried to be discrete but a doctor overheard one of our conversations and the sentiment of his comment to us was:

> "he will be lucky to be out of the hospital by the first of the month. I don't think he will be travelling to Switzerland any time soon."

The doctor knew what condition Jim's foot was in, but at that point, I had not seen it.

Jim's right foot had been amputated below the knee and he had been fitted with an immediate prosthesis. That was a blessing. If the doctors had not dealt so drastically with his left foot, he could have walked with crutches, and travelling would not have been so difficult. Instead, he travelled in a wheelchair—which was problematic with the small elevators in Europe.

He was released from the hospital less than a week before the trip, his right foot amputated and half of his left foot missing! Our friend, the podiatrist, provided a special shoe/boot for him to use to protect his foot from further damage while travelling.

On occasion, Philip, a friend of Jackie, played keyboards for the group. God allowed him to accompany Jim and the girls on the trip. Philip's Godly personality allowed him to be a servant, without whom, the trip would have been just about impossible. Even though Jim was in pain and very difficult to deal with, thank God, Philip was there just as if he were our son.

The audiences were absolutely mesmerized by the strength and conviction of Jims singing—from a wheelchair! All the while, no one could tell what he was going through or that he was in pain. That was the last time he sang publicly and I missed it. I should have gone with them.

Even then, I believed God was going to bring him out of this situation and allow him to rise again. God had been so faithful in keeping us from danger, both seen and unseen. However, that was my thinking, God had a different plan and it took the next several months to play out.

Once Jim came home from the tour, we had no choice but to agree to have his left foot amputated—gangrene had set in. We did not go back to the same hospital. The doctor at the new hospital said once the bone was exposed, saving the foot was impossible. The amount of tissue that had been removed would take years to regenerate, even on a healthy foot. The doctors at the new hospital were appalled that other doctors did what they had done to Jim's foot.

It was because of our decision to do it God's way, the Switzerland tour came to fruition. We did not shy away from the possibility of the trip being difficult. We did not know what was ahead for us so we were looking eagerly toward the future. The hair salon was almost a reality—we were not backing away from what was coming.

We can plan, but . . .

"We can make our plans, but the Lord determines our steps."

– Proverbs 16:9 NLT

A few months before Jim broke his hip, our youngest daughter, Jackie, began training to become a hair stylist. Jim promised to open a hair salon with her when she completed the course. Except her being his baby daughter, the one who makes the best glass of ice water, I do not know how she convinced him. That was the first time he seriously talked about it, much less considered opening another hair salon.

God most definitely does have a plan for our lives. I was not seeking God for a hair salon. Apparently Jim was. The owner of the building that housed the salon where Jim worked, called him. He was having a problem with the current tenant. He said he was tired of dealing with renters and he was interested in selling the building. God was working it out; we could open the salon as Jim had promised Jackie.

God blessed us to be able to take possession of the building right away. However, to be successful, the salon would have to be modernized. We met with the current tenants to tell them of the new ownership, explain the renovation, and give them thirty days notice. We knew everyone in the salon so we offered the stylists the opportunity to return when the renovations were completed. We expected the work would take about a month—in reality, it took a few weeks longer. When the renovations were completed, the stylists preferred to continue to work where they had moved. That salon was in worse shape than our salon before we renovated it. Oh well, their choice!

We could not afford to have a professional contractor do the work so it was up to me to turn the old salon into a thing of beauty. Thank God, our oldest daughter, Judy, and I enjoy doing renovation projects. We needed to turn a dark, outdated hair salon into an open, appealing space.

Avid fans of home improvement TV shows, Judy and I were up to the task. The structural bones in the building were good so there was very little work we could not do. Restructuring the space was not complicated. The most physically challenging part was removing the old partitions that enclosed each individual workstation. In the old salon, each workstation had a shampoo bowl within the workspace. The new design had a common shampoo area complete with extra dryers.

We updated the bathrooms with new fixtures—well, we did not personally change the fixtures but we changed the flooring in the bathrooms and did the painting that was needed throughout the salon.

The floors were nice—black and white asphalt tile squares laid on the diagonal. We replaced the commodes and hand bowls with white and finished with polished chrome fixtures. We replaced the 70's avocado green styling chairs and shampoo bowls with black. We replaced the assorted and old hair dryers with matching sets in black.

We painted the walls and wood paneling an ultra white and put a border at the ceiling. We surprised ourselves with our work and the finished project. Only God gave us the intelligence and ability to rearrange that space so well. When we were done, a dark, enclosed, outdated, wood-paneled hair salon was transformed into an open bright and airy space.

For the grand opening, some of Jim's clients had given us plants that added just the right touch of color and elegance.

Most of Jim's clientele came to the opening, I expect just to see him. The salon renovation was stunning and so was Jim—the salon in a good way; Jim, not so good. He had lost a little more than 100 pounds since any of his clients had seen him, nearly a year earlier. His complexion was dark; he had not been on dialysis long enough for the toxins to be cleared from his body. He was extremely weak and tired easily.

I think the grand opening of Sir James and Jackie Hair Salon ended Jim's desire to continue to press on. After all, he had lived up to his promise to Jackie. He had seen the salon, though he would never work in it, and he had provided some security for my future without him. I believe he was at peace with that part of his life.

Nearing the end

Jim was recuperating at a nursing home after his left foot was amputated. Although I was still skipping and tiptoeing through the tulips and refused to see it, he was failing quickly. His kidneys had begun to weaken even before the hip replacement surgery. The medicine to fight infection (for almost a year at that point) was wreaking havoc on almost every vital organ.

We decided Jim was not benefiting from being at the nursing home because he was too weak to do the therapy exercises. Having him at home was not a problem for me; making him comfortable was the priority.

Thank God, expense was not a concern, our health insurance covered everything we needed but Jim was an extremely personal person; a visiting nurse was not for him. I ordered all the equipment we needed and turned a spare room into Jim's new bedroom.

Jim's mother, affectionately called Grandma Rose, agreed to stay with us to help. I think she wanted to be near so she could oversee my care of Jim and to make sure he wanted for nothing.

At 85+ years, she was as agile as I was and her memory was better than most people half her age. Her help was perfect—she prepared meals for us and sat with Jim when I needed to run errands. Having him home was not a burden.

In the beginning, when he first broke his hip, he spent his free time reading, praying, and watching TV programs about nature. Overall, he was content. At that point, I think he believed he would recover completely. I certainly did. One of the last times I recall him walking, he came to dinner in the dining room twirling his cane on his hand, not using it for support. He had a big smile and he was walking with that confident swagger he did so well. Watching him cross the living room on his own steam was a beautiful sight.

Love does not seek its own

". . . does not behave rudely, does not seek its own, is not provoked, thinks no evil; does not rejoice in iniquity, but rejoices in truth; bears all things, believes all things, hopes all things, endures all things. "

— 1 Corinthians 13:5-7 NKJV

Many times I wondered if I loved Jim or if I were a fool. The 13th Chapter of 1 Corinthians affirms my love. I will not pretend to compare my love for him with the love that is spoken of in 1 Corinthians 13. However, my actions, for the most part, looked like the love described there.

During the many months I cared for him, I was not trying to prove my love, it just happened. When I looked around after everything was over, there it was; proof of my love for him in my caring for him. However, there was nothing in my heart to prove his love for me. My heart and virtually every other emotion had long since been dulled by his callous treatment of me. Throughout our marriage, I was systematically desensitized, partly of my own doing, in deference to Jim's points of view. I decided the struggle to express myself was not worth the effort I had to make to confront him. I do not know whether this makes me a coward. Even today, I will do a lot to avoid a confrontation. To me, confrontation is painful—I always suffer more than the person I am confronting. Over the years, I became conciliatory.

The emotional rape by Jim, along with the damage already done by family sent me in a loop that was not easily broken. The damage was layered slowly and methodically, therefore, a smooth, solid foundation was formed. By the time I realized I was in danger, I was uncomfortably close to collapse. I found I was a shell of a person, with no inner substance, nothing to draw on.

For years, I resembled a stepford wife. Being human, I could not possibly be perfect, but I did closely resemble perfection, in the natural, to anyone looking on. Appearances mattered, that was good enough for Jim.

In the book *The Stepford Wives*, by Ira Levine, the wives actually were robots. They were specifically programmed to be perfect for their husbands. The wives, literally, could not do anything that would be upsetting to their husbands. They were completely subservient, the perfect wife, mother and housekeeper, from the husbands point of view. Jim's motivation might have been the same as the husbands in the book—total unquestioning agreement with whatever he wanted. I do not know. He certainly did his part to groom me to be completely compliant to his wishes.

Rules were set early in our marriage. Being young and in love, there was nothing I would not do to please him. I became pregnant the first month we were married so when he asked me to call him when I got in from work, I took the request as concern for my well-being. Oh, he could be so charming! It never occurred to me calling him cleared his agenda for the rest of the evening. After my call, we normally did not speak again until he came home.

Jim played on my love for him, my innocence and naïveté. I believe he loved me as much as I loved him—just in a different way, the only way he knew to love. I guess what people say about men being from Mars and women being from Venus does have some credibility because looking back on our early years, nothing he told me made any sense.

For instance, just months into our marriage, when caught, he told me his philandering had nothing to do with me! Of course, I believed it was entirely my fault; my sexual innocence was the culprit. After a few weeks, when I finally stopped crying, I realized he was right; it really did not have anything to do with me. I guess philandering was not the word to use here. Sexual immorality is a more accurate description of what was going on.

I had just cause to chuck him in a nursing home and forget him. Instead, I cared for him as though he had been a morally perfect husband. As if I knew, if he were asked, he would choose me instead of Steve or John or Harry or Joe.

Fair warning

Jackie and James (yes, Jackie's husbands name is James also) were seeking prayer for themselves, James in particular, when they went to a healing service at a church, where the pastor is a prophet. A follow-up visit was customary, the pastor or someone from her staff would visit each person they prayed with. During the following week the Pastor, visited Jackie and James at their home. While she was visiting, she gave them a prophetic word about Jim, she said:

"He is going to die!"

Just like that! She hesitated then said:

"Yeah, he is going to die. You may as well get prepared because you all will need to stick together as a family."

That word was confirmation for Jackie. Before the prophecy was given she had a vision where Jim was already prepared for burial, laying in a casket. On the other hand, the prophecy was difficult for Judy to accept because without disrespecting the prophet, she could not believe God would take Jim's life because of his sinful ways. I am sure Judy was thinking:

"No, he is not perfect, but he has a good heart and he has done a lot to advance the kingdom of God. "

I believe Jesus had someone exactly like Jim in mind when he said:

"Not every one that saith unto me, Lord, Lord, shall enter into the kingdom of heaven; but he that doeth the will of my Father which is in heaven. Many will say to me in that day, Lord, Lord, have we not prophesied in thy name? and in thy name have cast out devils? and in thy name done many wonderful works?

And then will I profess unto them, I never knew you: depart from me, ye that work iniquity."

– Matthew 7:21-23

After praying about it, God led her, by the Holy Spirit, to a scripture that explained to her, God surely would do whatever He needs to do to win a soul. With that revelation, Judy sensed a fierce battle in the spirit realm for Jim's soul. Both God and Satan were vying for him. Each of them wanted his soul desperately as a trophy—someone each would relish as an ultimate victory.

Through the power of the Holy Spirit, Judy sensed Jim's anger with God for making him attracted to men. God revealed to her that love was Jim's motivation and Satan had taken his quest for the love of his father and twisted it until it became a perversion.

Jim had experienced a complication during one of his dialysis sessions and was hospitalized when Judy confronted him about being angry with God. I was not in the room, but I am sure tears filled his eyes. Her confrontation had to be a surprise and an embarrassment to him because the family never acknowledged that part of his life. Although, both Judy and Jackie later admitted they knew something was amiss with him. Judy soothed him and assured him that God did not make him that way.

Continuing to be led by the Holy Spirit, she told him his desire for men was a twisted and perverted ploy by Satan. She further explained that God is love and love was the real motivation for his lifestyle. In seeking men, he was not looking for sex; he was looking for the love he never got from his father. That day, he was delivered and healed as he talked with Judy. That was the last obstacle Jim had to face that any of us could help him work through.

Last few months

During the last few months of his life, he was able to develop a strong relationship with God. Jim grew weaker physically and more strong spiritually.

Before he became too weak and disoriented, we talked about the pain he had caused me with his behavior and his general disregard for our marriage. He asked me to forgive him and promised he would never again subject me to such treatment. I said I forgave him and I thought I meant it, but somewhere in my mind, I was still expecting him to rebound and become the old Jim again. I had not really forgiven him or myself for allowing him to mistreat me so long. His apology started me doubting my self-worth.

A typical morning was to get Jim fed, bathed, and the bed changed. After about a month of changing the bed and washing Jim repeatedly within hours, I decided his pride would have to suffer, I began to use diapers. This would not have been a problem except he was so vain. Before using diapers, keeping up with the laundry was a full-time occupation. Everything, pajamas, sheets and blankets had to be soaked before they could be washed.

Thinking about this now, I realize this phase in his illness had to be extremely hard for him—not only because he had been so vain, but because of his treatment of me over the years. Now, I was the one on whom he depended. Only once, near the end, did revenge enter my mind. Almost as quickly as it came, I rebuked the thought and went on with whatever it was I was doing for him.

I stumbled upon Romans 12:19-21 as I was looking for a passage I knew about, in Proverbs. I wanted to quote the text in Proverbs to explain what I thought Jim must have been feeling was biblical. Maybe even expound on the idea that we should be careful how we treat people. That was not where God wanted me to go. Instead, He led me to write, if we love, as God intends us, we will do what is right for everyone and when we no longer can care for ourselves, the same love we gave will come back to us. We will not have to be concerned with feeling burning coals being heaped on our heads.

> *"Do not take revenge, my friends, but leave room for God's wrath, for it is written: It is mine to avenge; I will repay, says the Lord. On the contrary: If your enemy is hungry, feed him; if he is thirsty, give him something to drink. In doing this, you will heap burning*

coals on his head. ' Do not be overcome by evil, but overcome evil with good"

– Romans 12:19-21 NIV

The prize is in view

For the first time, I faced it—Jim was dying. He had been diagnosed with three illnesses, any of which could end his life at any time. His doctors told us in addition to diabetes and high blood pressure, he had congestive heart failure, kidney failure and prostate cancer. I don't remember what I was told about the cause of the seizures and strokes he was experiencing.

The last trip to the hospital was because of a complication during dialysis. Jim told me he wanted to stop dialysis because it was making him sicker. He said he never wanted to go to the hospital again; he just wanted to go home.

Three of the four times we moved, as a family, Jim was working and did not help pack or unpack. He was excited and anxious about our last move. As we unpacked, I thought he was just weary when he said, "Never again; I am never moving again. They will carry me out of here". I wonder if he knew and chose not to share!

We talked about stopping dialysis. I wanted to be sure he knew what he was asking. I reminded him of his aunt who refused dialysis, he said he understood and that was what he wanted. Jim's understanding of not having dialysis was that death was just round the corner. I think he chose to be home at the end.

The patient liaison at the hospital helped us get hospice involved. That made the end easier for me. Otherwise, because he would be at home when he died, there would have to be an investigation and possibly an autopsy to rule out foul play. She discussed the entire procedure with Jim and me to be sure that was what he wanted. She explained that at the end, all I would have to do was call hospice. They would take care of the details from there.

Jim began having seizures a few months before he started dialysis and Dilantin was prescribed to control them. The medicine caused a rash that looked just awful. A dark, crusty rash covered his entire body. The doctors changed the medicine but it had been weeks and the rash was still quite visible. A week or so after stopping dialysis, the rash cleared up completely. His complexion was clear and his skin was soft and smooth again.

I like to believe when Jim decided he wanted to go home, he did not mean our house, he meant to his heavenly home.

The week before his death, Jim's appetite was good, and he was active. He asked the girls to sing a song none of them recognized from the few words he remembered. As it turned out, they did know the hymn. He used "Keep me Every Day", by F. I. Eiland and Emmet S. Dean, as his final testimony, declaring his total dependence on God and his faith in Gods sustaining power:

> *"Lord, I want to live for Thee, Every day and hour;*
> *Let Thy Spirit be with me, In its saving power!*
> *Keep my heart, and keep my hand, Keep my soul, I pray!*
> *Keep my tongue to speak Thy praise, Keep me all the way!"*

The Thursday before his death, he ate about half a medium size apple and sang the chorus of a song to a family friend.

On Friday morning, he said he did not want anything to eat and he did not want to be bathed. He folded his hands at his groin and went to sleep. He never woke from that sleep. About 24 hours later, he simply stopped breathing; he was ready—no drama, no chaos.

His body may have been retaining fluids, but he looked as if he had gained weight. Looking at the shell he left behind, no one could see what he had gone through. He seemed to be asleep when God took him, peacefully with his family gathered around his bed.

None of us, Jim, Judy, Jackie, nor I backed up, thank God! We, each of us, stepped up when it was our turn to make a difference. Each of us had choices and we all forged ahead.

Jim could have stayed home and not gone to Switzerland. No one would have blamed him. If he had not gone on the tour, many people would have missed the gospel he presented. He did not back up. He sowed into the wind. We will never know how bountiful the harvest is from the seeds he sowed. At that time, the messenger was flawed, not the message.

Who would blame Judy if she had not confronted her father about his hatred for God—and on such a sensitive subject! We can rest assured; Jim's eternal future would not have been so bright if Judy had backed up.

Jackie, being the youngest, certainly could have been intimidated enough to refuse to pass the prophetic message to Jim. However, if she had backed up, Jim would have missed precious time to prepare himself to meet God. He could have missed the opportunity and lost the battle!

It never occurred to me to do less than I did for Jim. My vow to him, and God was 'in sickness and in health'. I loved him in all the ways love exists—love bears all things. . . love endures all things.

Part 3

And when you cannot see
your way through, definitely

But when you ask him, be sure that your faith is in God alone. Do not waver, for a person with divided loyalty is as unsettled as a wave of the sea that is blown and tossed by the wind. Such people should not expect to receive anything from the Lord. Their loyalty is divided between God and the world, and they are unstable in everything they do.

– James 1:6-8 NLT

Don't Blink

We must keep the faith for many reasons, but the reason we cannot blink is that it is impossible to please God if we are wavering in our beliefs—blinking! Confidence in God is grounded in character, but building character is not easily, nor is it quickly achieved. It takes time and patience.

Check Yourself

Some people are blessed enough to see themselves when one day they pass a mirror and instead of seeing their reflection, they see greed, anger, jealousy or other qualities not normally visible in a mirror. Only after sin is identified can it be confronted and exposed. Then, with the help of the Holy Spirit, the root spirit that controls the sin can be evicted.

Life has thrown me a few curves. I thank God; my trials made my life better, and through my testimony, will make your life better as well. I can assure you—you are stronger than you know and you are not alone. I want to help you understand, you will endure. All you have to do is learn not to blink! It is true, God will not put more on you than you can tolerate. So, if you are going through a trial, it is to make you stronger. Thank Him! It is not to harm you but to help you align yourself with God.

I went through many trials before I learned I had to change before things would get better! I could not recognize my part because I was not willing to admit and accept responsibility for the mess in my life.

I found when I examine myself first situations do not seem so unjust. The wish-a-could-a-should-a thoughts that run through my mind help me formulate prayers for resolution to begin with me. I ask God to change my will to His. Try it! It will work for you as it has for me. The only thing you will lose is an annoyed spirit. You will gain the ability to look Satan in the eye without blinking.

My goal was to see myself as God sees me. When I asked God to see myself, I got nothing or so I thought. The suppression practice that had worked so well began to fail me—my mind ran out of space.

You see, all my life, I was continuously packing my emotions inside and not allowing them any freedom. Each time I suppressed an emotion, I was adding a brick to the wall that surrounded my character.

But God! To protect my sanity, He allowed individual parts of my personality to be visible, but not to me. God knows what each individual will best respond to. For me, He knew it would be almost impossible for me to see my faults, so He arranged a little help for me. I displayed multiple personalities (Dissociative Identity Disorder) as a coping mechanism for survival.

The weight of not being aware of differences in my behavior, never knowing when my actions were inappropriate or offensive made me withdraw within myself. When the despicable personality showed up at church, I sought professional help. My doctor helped me understand the origin of my various personalities. Thank God, if there was a personality who was my protector, she/he never attacked anyone. I don't think any of them showed signs of being vicious or aggressive. Even so, some people who were around me frequently were afraid for their safety. Others felt I was so out of order, to be with me was toxic to them.

I had little or no natural affection for anyone. It came as a shock to me when I realized, I did not even know how to love. Warm hugs and kisses, pats on the back, and general acknowledgment that I was alive had not been a part of my upbringing. Though I was saved at a young age, I did not have the love of God in me! The thirteenth chapter of 1 Corinthians, summed up my problem.

*"And if I have prophetic powers (the gift of interpreting the divine
will and purpose), and understand all the secret truths and mysteries
and possess all knowledge, and if I have [sufficient] faith so that I
can remove mountains, but have not love (God's love in me) I am
nothing (a useless nobody). "*

– 1 Corinthians 13:2 AMP

This new status was difficult for me to accept—remember, I did not
think of myself as a hardcore sinner—I was not a thief, a murderer, or
a whoremonger. I lived, what I considered a respectable life. It never
occurred to me having a hard heart was a problem. Nor did letting
words flow from my mouth that hurt others cause a problem for me, if
I did not use profanity.

My life evolved to a point where I was not comfortable talking to
people for fear I would be misunderstood. One personality called to
my attention was so repulsive to me, the thought of her being a part of
me, was unbearable. My priority became centered on getting rid of
all of the personalities—by whatever means necessary. I knew I was in
deep trouble when death seemed the better alternative to what others
were seeing. I had to find a way to rid myself of those personalities,
without taking my life. I listed the habits I wanted to change and added
the personality traits I was told about to the list. Taking a clue from the
format used by Germaine Copeland in her book, *Prayers that Avail
Much,* I searched the scriptures until I found texts that spoke positively
to each area I needed help with.

𝒦nock the wall down

Thank God, through the power of the Holy Spirit, each of the personalities
helped me demolish the wall that surrounded me. Their presence
helped me develop a prayer; the wall was destroyed, brick by brick,
through the following prayer:

*Father, it is difficult to put into words how I feel during this
time. I seem so out of touch with everyone, even myself. I
feel as though I am in a vacuum. My head seems empty,
I have no good thoughts, no ideas, no desires, no wants,*

no dreams, and there is nothing creative or constructive present in my thinking. In the name of Jesus, I pray the following requests will undergo a divine, supernatural germination seedtime and harvest, which will manifest itself during this season.

Please God, grant me:

A relationship with You, O Lord that will:

➤ Instill in me a natural desire to stay away from willful sins

> *"Keep your servant also from willful sins; may they not rule over me. Then will I be blameless, innocent of great transgression".*

> *— Psalm 19:13 NIV*

➤ Show me how to monitor my mouth and heart so compassion is always on my lips and in my heart

> *"May the words of my mouth and the meditation of my heart be pleasing in your sight, O LORD, my Rock and my Redeemer. "*

> *— Psalm 19:14 NIV*

➤ Clothe me with strength and dignity without being prideful

> *"She is clothed with strength and dignity;"*

> *— Proverbs 31:25a NIV*

➤ Show me how to take good care of my body

> *"Flee from sexual immorality. All other sins a man commits are outside his body, but he who sins sexually sins against his own body. Do you not know that your body is a temple of the Holy Spirit, who is in you, whom you have received from God? You are not your own; you were bought at a price. Therefore honor God with your body"*

> *— 1 Corinthians 6:18-20 NIV*

Oh God, give me the agility of mind to:

> *Express myself clearly without rambling*
> *Evaluate and assess situations*
> *Think quickly*
> *Think clearly*
> *Allow me to have a naturally good sense of humor without*
> *offending anyone or belittling anyone*

Father, allow the fruit of the Holy Spirit to abound in me and make Himself visible in the way I live:

> *"But the fruit of the Spirit is love, joy, peace, patience, kindness, goodness, faithfulness, gentleness and self-control"*
>
> *– Galatians 5:22-23a NIV*

➤ Give me a clean heart that will let me love others with deeds, not just words but with actions and truth

> *"Create in me a pure heart, O God, Psalm 51:10a NIV; Dear children, let us not love with words or tongue but with actions and in truth. "*
>
> *– 1 John 3:18 NIV*

➤ Let me experience the joy of a righteous and upright heart

> *"Light is shed upon the righteous and joy on the upright in heart. "*
>
> *– Psalm 97:11 NIV*

➤ Discipline me Father, so I may be righteous and at peace.

> *"No discipline seems pleasant at the time, but painful. Later on, however, it produces a harvest of righteousness and peace for those who have been trained by it. "*
>
> *– Hebrews 12:11 NIV*

> ➤ *Anoint me Lord to have a calm spirit, one not easily provoked*

> *"A hot-tempered man stirs up dissension, but a patient man calms a quarrel. "*

> *– Proverbs 15:18 NIV*

Give me a spirit to do more than is asked of me—allow me to cheerfully help on all occasions.

> *"See, I am standing beside this spring, and the daughters of the townspeople are coming out to draw water. May it be that when I say to a girl, 'Please let down your jar that I may have a drink,' and she says, 'Drink, and I'll water your camels too' . . . "*

> *– Genesis 24:13-14 NIV*

Allow me to live as a child of the light, where the light shows in all goodness—where I know what pleases the Lord

> *"For you were once darkness, but now you are light in the Lord. Live as children of light "for the fruit of the light consists in all goodness, righteousness and truth and find out what pleases the Lord. "*

> *– Ephesians 5:8-10 NIV*

Bind faithfulness about my neck and put love in my heart

> *"Let love and faithfulness never leave you; bind them around your neck, write them on the tablet of your heart."*

> *– Proverbs 3:3 NIV*

Help me understand how to clothe myself in gentleness

> *"Therefore, as God's chosen people, holy and dearly loved, clothe yourselves with compassion, kindness, humility, gentleness and patience. "*

> *– Colossians 3:12 NIV*

Endow me with self control:

> ➤ Give me the sense to know when I should reject things

> > *"But Daniel resolved not to defile himself with the royal food and wine, and he asked the chief official for permission not to defile himself this way. "*
> >
> > *– Daniel 1:8 NIV*

> ➤ and when I have had enough

> > *"If you find honey, eat just enough—too much of it, and you will vomit. "*
> >
> > *– Proverbs 25:16 NIV*

Grant me the grace to get wisdom and understanding

> *"Wisdom is the principal thing; therefore get wisdom: and with all thy getting get understanding. "*
>
> *– Proverbs 4:7*

Father, activate the gifts already given to me

> ➤ by the Holy Spirit:

> > *"Now to each one the manifestation of the Spirit is given for the common good. To one there is given through the Spirit the message of wisdom, to another the message of knowledge by means of the same Spirit, to another faith by the same Spirit, to another gifts of healing by that one Spirit, to another miraculous powers, to another prophecy, to another distinguishing between spirits, to another speaking in different kinds of tongues and to still another the interpretation of tongues. All these are the work of one and the same Spirit, and he gives them to each one, just as he determines."*
> >
> > *– 1Corinthians 12:7-11 NIV*

➢ by the Son:

> "It was he who gave some to be apostles, some to be
> prophets, some to be evangelists, and some to be pastors
> and teachers,"

– Ephesians 4:11 NIV

➢ And by the Father:

> "If you preach, just preach God's Message, nothing else;
> if you help, just help, don't take over; if you teach, stick
> to your teaching; if you give encouraging guidance, be
> careful that you don't get bossy; if you're put in charge,
> don't manipulate; if you're called to give aid to people in
> distress, keep your eyes open and be quick to respond; if
> you work with the disadvantaged, don't let yourself get
> irritated with them or depressed by them. Keep a smile
> on your face."

– Romans 12:6-8 MSG

*Please Father, grant me a calm, sincere, and peace loving
countenance at all times*

> "But the wisdom that comes from heaven is first of all
> pure; then peace-loving, considerate, submissive, full of
> mercy and good fruit, impartial and sincere."

– James 3:17 NIV

All these blessings I ask in the precious name of Jesus, Amen.

After praying this prayer, morning and night for several days, the
discomfort of seeing myself eased up. The comfort of knowing I had
actually come through a really rough patch of time, was energizing.
That is putting it mildly. From this realization, I gathered strength to press
on toward to the high calling of Christ!

Parallel lives

God reminded me that several people, over the past few years, had
commented either directly to me or in my presence, on the metamorphosis

of the Caterpillar. It felt good to hear—one day I was going to be free and beautiful. But, until now, I could not relate. I did not know or care anything about caterpillars, except they turned into butterflies. I began to study the life cycle of caterpillars—as I did, God was right in my ear whispering:

"See, that's what you have been going through".

My life had been paralleling the life cycle of a caterpillar! The analogy was mind blowing. Caterpillars enclose themselves in a cocoon. I built my cocoon from childhood. They build it slowly and methodically to completely enclose and protect themselves as they are molded into a new being. If anyone, recognizing the struggle of the caterpillar, attempts to break the cocoon for the caterpillar, it will die. No one could give me what I needed during my remolding—I was in it alone. The caterpillar enclosed itself and it must free itself. Now that it is over and I am free, I can say, it was a battle well worth fighting.

As I compared myself to a caterpillar, I noticed I dropped fleshy thoughts and desires from my life as I grew spiritually. As I dropped those parts of me that were hindering my growth, there was a struggle but I grew more each time something was shed.

Then there came a point in my development when I was completely disoriented. I was hurt. I felt abandoned. I was depressed. I was weak. I thought no one understands what I am going through or even cares. I equate this period in my life with the pupa of the caterpillar.

During the Pupa stage for a caterpillar, it attaches itself, upside down to a twig, sheds its final exoskeleton, and grows its new shell or cocoon. Inside this cocoon, the caterpillar undergoes a change in which the old shape of the caterpillar is broken down and reshaped into that of a butterfly.

During this breaking and reforming, the caterpillar seems to be dead. Through this dormant period, the final stage of the caterpillar, blood is being pumped to the head and thorax of the transformed butterfly. The head expands until it cracks the shell and the butterfly is then able to work its way free. A few hours after coming out of the cocoon, the wings become dry and the butterfly is ready to fly—transformation is complete.

When my transformation began, everyone close to me knew something was going on. However, no one could help me! I can only assume they recognized trying to help me would do more harm than good. That stage was difficult for me to accept; no one was going to try to help me out of the dark enclosure that encircled me. I felt as if everyone could see me in that deep, dark hole yet no one was willing to help me out of it. I felt completely abandoned.

At that point, I decided I needed to know what the Bible had to say about my situation. I began to read and study the Bible more often—every morning as part of my morning devotional. Reading and studying God's Word was filling my head and heart to saturation. I did not get entire revelations on anything in particular, but I did get clarity on how to handle problems in general. Continue, relentlessly, to study God's word and pray, not looking to any human for advice or comfort. As I studied and prayed, I received new understanding. I, like the caterpillar, was shedding layers that no longer fit. Each time I shed a layer in the natural, I grew stronger in the spirit.

In order to shed the last layer, I went through stressful psychological changes. It was during that time my several other personalities (with the help of the Holy Spirit) worked with me and began to break down the wall I started building as a child. As portions of the wall were demolished, personalities disappeared.

Now I had God, Jesus, and the Holy Spirit to comfort, protect and provide for me. The realization that I no longer needed the various personalities took time to sink in. As that truth settled in, so did the confident assurance that what I want to happen is going to happen. I became sure, what I was hoping for, was waiting for me, though I could not see it.

Attaining this new awareness was my drying period. Just as the wings of the butterfly have to dry before she can fly, I had to trust God totally before my change could be complete.

I am now a beautiful butterfly—completely changed, inside and out. Changed from a worm, crawling on its belly, to a colorful, winged being that soars and partakes of nectar from flowers.

Inside the cocoon

As I shed old habits and wrong ways of thinking, it became clear to me that my character was changing. Extraordinary changes were occurring as I started to build the character God expects His servants to have. Ordinary things you might not notice will make you blink—without a second thought. Some of these things include jealousy, speaking to someone rudely, self-will and lack of self-discipline. These and several other idiosyncrasies or 'just my ways' played a part in influencing others around me. Habits I had developed over many years, my way of thinking and assessing situations made me blink, and often. It took some time and lots of thought to see that *everybody* can't be wrong.

Jealousy

Being left out of something you want to be a part of is possibly the worst feeling in the world.

I do not think I am a jealous person—but I have felt true jealousy at least once in my life. Initially, I did not know what it was. It seemingly overshadowed me. I felt as though I could not breathe. There was no light around me, although it was midmorning on a summer day. It was the worst feeling I have ever had, and there was nothing I could do about it. There was no escape from that sensation, it was pure torture. It caused paranoia. I thought no one cared about me. I accused everyone of deliberately avoiding me because they just wanted to be mean to me.

You may be surprised to know what an insignificant thing it was that caused me an entire day of agony—I could not reach Judy or Jackie. I was jealous because they were taping a performance for an internationally known Gospel music TV show and they did not invite me to come along!!!

Jealousy told me: though they normally would have talked to me before going to the taping, neither of them bothered because they did not want to include me. Jealousy would not let me understand anything except, I was left out.

Gideon and Jephthah

Look at Gideon and Jephthah for prime examples of jealousy. The men of Ephraim wanted to be included with Gideon and Jephthah in the battles they fought. The accounts of these incidents are in the book of Judges.

Gideon quelled hard feelings when he reminded the leaders of Ephraim that they actually caught the leaders of the Midianites. It was impressive during that period, to capture and kill the leaders during a battle. Gideon gave the Ephraimites the glory for the battle and the feeling of being left out was avoided.

Jephthah, on the other hand, was not so diplomatic. The Ephraimites jealousy caused the death of many of their own men. Their jealousy caused them to insult Jephthah and his men. Both groups were wrong. The Ephraimites were at fault because they allowed jealousy to shape their actions—Jephthah was at fault because he allowed the Ephraimites' insults to anger him to the point of rage.

Jealousy will feast on insecurity; it can only fast in the company of confidence in God. Jealousy could not feast on Gideon because he knew, without any doubt, the victory belonged to God. All Gideon did was follow Gods instructions to the victory.

In my case, jealousy had a feast because I was insecure. I was blinking—believing I had been abandoned. The spirit of rejection reigned that day. But thank God, since that day, I learned about spiritual warfare. That spirit has been evicted, thank you Jesus.

Not if, but when a situation comes up, will jealousy have a feast on you or will it have to fast?

Self-will

Self-will must go before God will use anyone for His purposes. God will crush self-will to establish a faithful and obedient servant who is willing to do whatever He requires, immediately upon request. If Jesus had to give up His (human) will when He was called to die for my sins, I have to submit. Things must be this way so God gets all the glory. There can be no way anyone can assume any credit for God's work.

There is no 'I did it my way' on this journey. I have surrendered my will. I actually begged God to mold my will to fit His. Many times I tell God, although I want 'that', I really only want what He wants me to have. Not always, but sometimes, my desire changes. I always have peace on the matter because I know Gods way is best.

When my will is in harmony with His, I can be in His presence with comfort. After all, what I want most is to be in His presence, because in His presence there is fullness of joy, on His right, pleasures forever. When I indulge self-will I am not blinking, my eyes are completely shut.

Self-discipline:
Little foxes that spoil the vine

It is me, oh Lord! It is easy to overlook a small faux pas—especially when it involves an established routine. A faux pas is a minor mistake in etiquette, one that will not cause harm to anyone but may cause embarrassment. You know the kind of behavior a spoiled child may be guilty of.

Proverbs 23:13 says to spare the rod is to spoil the child. Some may look on using the rod as cruel while others understand what is going on because they love, truly love their children. To me, this premise is not so much about applying the physical rod, as it is to deal with the problem. We can see this if we take a look at what I believe are the reasons for this scripture:

1) *to prevent building a routine behavior, and*

2) *to develop self-discipline.*

A two-year-old has almost no self-discipline. Whatever he wants to do is OK with him. However, if parents do not correct their children and show them what type of behavior is allowed, the children will grow, building routines that condone less self-discipline. In other words, become spoiled.

Spoiled is an interesting label we use, and is entirely appropriate. When we think of something spoiled, we think of something rotten, no good for anything. From that viewpoint, it is difficult to look at oneself and admit being spoiled. In my case, it was true and hard for me to recognize in myself.

What could be wrong with a behavior I have indulged for many years? I could not see it—no discernment to help me. As early as I can clearly remember, I have gotten what I wanted by asking someone in power to give 'it' to me—not always even saying thank you!

Today, I am convinced my parents and siblings encouraged that spoiled behavior. Older parents who just wanted me to be comfortable and quiet; siblings who thought my behavior was cute. Years of indulging that lack of self-discipline produced an impatient, demanding and immature personality.

My character was non-existent with regard to selfishness. The odd thing about this little fox is, I could never see him. He could have been a wart on my nose, but because he was there so long, he became invisible to me. Everyone else could see, but to me, my spoiled behavior was just a part of the landscape of my life. Because I try to be pleasant to others, no one would tell me I was selfish—I would not have believed it if they did.

You see, this is one of the reasons I needed the Holy Spirit to be active in my life, so He could unstop my ears, open my eyes and adjust my mind to be receptive to all the spoiled attributes in my life. Without Him, I could have stumbled around blind, mute, and with little reasoning ability much longer than I did. Thank you Jesus for dying for me so I might have free access to the Holy Spirit and His willingness to correct me when I blink.

Eyes wide open—shut—no open

"So also, the tongue is a small thing, but what enormous damage it can do. A tiny spark can set a great forest on fire"

– James 3:5 TLB

The tongue is a little member but its power and influence are mighty! Another little fox – "Oh, I was just kidding"! Were you really? Growing up unchallenged in making sarcastic remarks led me to a life of double mindedness. It became increasingly difficult to decide what I truly meant and how I truly felt on any subject. You may have heard, God wants no part of a double-minded person. Therefore, a double-minded person gets nothing from God.

"That man should not think he will receive anything from the Lord; he is a double-minded man, unstable in all he does."

– James 1:7-8 NIV

God is good. Until I realized I was double-minded and had horrible habits because of it, God did not hold me accountable (at least not that I can now recognize). It is a completely different story since my eyes are open and my understanding enlarged. The Holy Spirit convicts me at every infraction and helps me correct that behavior.

Misunderstanding

"May the words of my mouth and the meditation of my heart be pleasing in your sight, O LORD, my Rock and my Redeemer."

– Psalm 19:14 NIV

Being misunderstood has encouraged me to look for ways to express myself that are outside my box. I am constantly aware of what and how I am communicating. I must be certain my feelings and motivation are in tune with the Holy Spirit. I must lean and depend on the Holy Spirit of God to prepare my heart, body language, and mouth to communicate what He would have me communicate, for His glory and to the building of His kingdom. Moreover, even after all those precautions, people closest to me will misunderstand—those will be humbling experiences. In order to have those experiences become learning experiences, I have to be in prayer constantly, so I am free from bitterness and unforgiveness.

Patience

"I waited patiently for the LORD; He turned to me and heard my cry."

– Psalm 40:1 NIV

I have indeed surrendered all to Jesus and I am waiting for His time. I have learned to wait patiently on Him. I have endured hard times and learned not to complain. I have learned to bear pain and endure trouble without making a fuss—God knows I have learned that His ways and timing are always best. In everything I do, I defer my will and selfish goals to allow His will to be done. He knows how old I am so whatever He asks of me is do-able in my lifetime and it will not only bless me but others as well.

Frustration

Frustration, for me, is sneaky. One day I look up and everything seems useless and unfruitful. Nothing is going as planned and everything takes twice as long as I thought to accomplish. Then, when I finally say to myself, 'you coulda had a V8', I realize I did not pray before I started my day. More likely, I remember I haven't studied the Word in several days. Just reading a verse or two daily is not enough for me to survive. Immediately after a quality study period, everything is in focus and on track again. When we are frustrated, we are blinking!

Discouragement

"But thou, O LORD, art a shield for me; my glory, and the lifter up of mine head. "

– Psalm 3:3

During times of discouragement, I cannot afford to go away and hide from God. I run to Him in prayer and have meals of scripture to sustain me. Constant prayer, face-to-face dialogue with God, result in instructions from God on what to do. At one point, nothing I did came out right. That was before I learned to always be in close contact with God. Many years ago, He told me His Word is a lamp to my feet and a light to my path. I did not understand what He was saying until much later.

It is difficult to stay discouraged when following God. He deflects the arrows Satan intends for us. He encourages us by showing us where we are headed and He tells us what the outcome will be. This protection is available when instructions are coming directly from God, through the Holy Bible.

Spiritual Warfare

Spiritual warfare is experienced by everyone willing to align his thoughts and will with that of God. The battle must be fought with spiritual weapons—the Word, prayer, praise, and the name of the Lord Jesus Christ. Without spiritual warfare, we would not grow stronger in the spirit. We must never attempt to fight a spiritual fight in the natural.

I struggle on the battlefield of my mind daily. A few people automatically provoke judgmental thoughts by me. I cannot let any occurrence pass without fighting back, by rejecting the thought, and asking forgiveness from God. Since learning to fight, I find these occurrences are fewer and less intense. I have noticed that attacks come when I am weak. Staying spiritually and physically fit is necessary so when Satan comes to rattle the doors and windows of my mind; I am ready for him, not blinking.

Vision

Without spiritual vision, I will not know the will of God. Natural vision is of no use in spiritual situations. God's will is only revealed through the Holy Spirit and to know His will, I must constantly be in touch with Him.

Sometimes I am spiritually blind as a bat, but my prayer for me is that God will give me an increasingly discerning heart—the spiritual wisdom to see what lies before me.

These are a few of the challenges I faced as my spirit was being remolded. I am still a work in progress and will be until I die. Any of these concerns may revisit me and maybe even trip me up. We all fall; the trick is to recognize the test and quickly get back up.

Part 4

After you've done all you can—

And that about wraps it up. God is strong, and he wants you strong. So take everything the Master has set out for you, well-made weapons of the best materials. And put them to use so you will be able to stand up to everything the Devil throws your way. This is no afternoon athletic contest that we'll walk away from and forget about in a couple of hours. This is for keeps, a life-or-death fight to the finish against the Devil and all his angels.

Be prepared. You're up against far more than you can handle on your own. Take all the help you can get, every weapon God has issued, so that when it's all over but the shouting you'll still be on your feet. Truth, righteousness, peace, faith, and salvation are more than words. Learn how to apply them. You'll need them throughout your life. God's Word is an indispensable weapon. In the same way, prayer is essential in this ongoing warfare. Pray hard and long. Pray for your brothers and sisters. Keep your eyes open. Keep each other's spirits up so that no one falls behind or drops out.

– Ephesians 6:10-18 MSG

Stand

I can say facing my problems from a Godly perspective has always worked and I have no regrets. At the end of the day, I am at peace with God and family because I stand on what my parents instilled in me as a child. Nothing they taught me made me impervious to hard knocks. However, their teaching prepared me for life, in that it gave me something to believe in, something to hold onto. It made me similar to the punching toy that refuses to stay knocked down. You can punch it hard as you like but it comes back upright.

Something at the bottom of the toy anchors it and weighs it down. That's it! My parents weighed me down with God, truth, fidelity and the value of a good name. With these characteristics grounding me, I stand upright and only wobble when hit. When the storm passes and the dust settles, I am standing. My parents missed a few things in my upbringing—things other parents do naturally, but I thank you Jesus for those good things my imperfect parents did impart to me.

I have been led to share my story with people who cannot bring themselves to talk about intimate things that go on in their marriages. For some, the abuse may be so subtle they may not realize it is happening. Some snap under pressure and resort to violence to fix the problems they face daily. Others dissolve the marriage and keep going, without having learning anything positive. Then they repeat the pattern two, maybe three times before they get it. We should be able to learn from one another. I suffered, you don't have to.

The lessons I learned helped stabilize my life. No, I do not believe I have been so out of God's will that He needed to punish me. However, I have been so loved by Him and at the same time, so out of His will—He decided to help me regain my equilibrium and stand.

First Lesson

The first lesson I want to impress on you is never to lose faith in God. Hold on, whatever the cost. Even when you cannot see what He is leading you into, just believe He is sovereign and He knows what He is doing. He is preparing a path for you to achieve what you desire but cannot see. He is preparing a path you would not have chosen for yourself because it looks too rocky and hard. Think about this, if the path were smooth, without ruts, would you ever appreciate the smooth path? It was only after a rough time that I could appreciate the times when everything was handed to my family and me. Without jolts from pitfalls, I never would have come out of that state of oblivion where I ignored God and all He was doing in my life.

I had no pressing need to be in touch with Him, to thank Him for His goodness, to seek His guidance, or to just enjoy being in His presence. Thank You Jesus, through it all, I did learn to depend on Him. I also learned I was not deserving of anything because of my goodness, but because of His mercy.

Keep the faith you have in God, however little you think that may be. Trust God to help you strengthen that portion, in Him. Pray He will use your faith as He did with Rahab, but remember, others trusted God and were killed rather than turn from Him—knowing they would rise to a better life afterward.

Second lesson

The second lesson is never to give in to what seems an adverse situation; even when you can see (in the natural) your circumstances are changing for the worse. That would be the time to pray for God to give you insight into what He is doing. More than likely, He will not give you the entire plan, but He will give you enough to calm your doubts and fears. Know that God controls everything and He has a plan.

If Jim and I had begun to look at our circumstances before he went to Switzerland and before we opened the hair salon, we probably would have given up and decided it was impossible. What person not believing in God would have attempted to go on a concert tour in Switzerland with one foot amputated six weeks before, and the other foot so badly mutilated, it could not be walked on? Who would attempt to renovate a building and open a hair salon on a budget less than $10,000?

I know Jim loved the Lord with all his heart. I believe he asked God for favor so he could have these last two achievements: open the hair salon and sing the Gospel of Jesus Christ at the Chéserex Jazz Festival in Montreux, Switzerland. The Gospel should be sung with enthusiasm, dancing, and celebration—how was he going to do that from a wheelchair? I was not there, but the report was that Jim was able to deliver the good news with gusto and even stood, briefly, during one of the concerts. Jim's success was an example of how God works for those who love Him and believe He can do all things!

I had to make a stand on the salon; I could not look at what I had to work with. I would not even begin to count resources. Judy and I just jumped in and began the process. Each need was addressed as it came up. God was always there with what we needed—when we needed it. Family members helped demolish the partitions that separated the styling spaces. Judy had a friend who cleaned the many layers of wax from the floor to reveal the beauty that had been hidden for years. Other friends and family helped with the plumbing— installing the new commodes, hand bowls and fixtures. In other words, do not believe what you see in the natural—believe with God, all things are possible!

Third lesson

When you cannot see how you can get through the current trial, do not waste time wavering between two opinions—work on your character. Get to know yourself and Gods will.

Destroy anything that stands between you and God. This may require a caterpillar experience. It may be you who has to be destroyed—broken and reshaped into a new being. It will be painful, but what a privilege to be molded by God, for His purpose. Remember, in your weakness, God, who is in control, is strong.

> *"But he said to me, "My grace is sufficient for you, for my power is made perfect in weakness. " Therefore I will boast all the more gladly about my weaknesses, so that Christ's power may rest on me. "*
>
> *– 2 Corinthians 12:9 NIV*

So, why would I bare my personal business, and embarrassing family secrets? Why would I air this laundry so candidly? There is only one reason—to comfort someone who may feel as alone and abandoned as I have felt.

> *"Arise, shine; for thy light is come, and the glory of the LORD is risen upon thee.*
>
> *For, behold, the darkness shall cover the earth, and gross darkness the people: but the LORD shall arise upon thee, and his glory shall be seen upon thee. "*
>
> *– Isaiah 60:1-2*

I assure you, God is there and He sees you. Now, you have to see Him and know He is in control. You have to know whatever you are going through is temporary.

If you want it, His Glory will rise on and overshadow you. Just ask Him. I did. This book is how His Glory shines through me. Thank You, Jesus!